THRIVE

with God

GALE ALVAREZ

THRIVE
with God

GALE ALVAREZ

WORD & SPIRIT
PUBLISHING

Copyright © 2020/2021 Gale Alvarez

All rights reserved. No part of this book may be used or reproduced by any means, graphic, electronic, or mechanical, including photocopying, recording, taping, or by any information storage retrieval system without the written permission of the author except in the case of brief quotations embodied in critical articles and reviews.

The author back cover photo was photographed by Albaner C. Eugene Jr. Transcription of the Facebook Live Video, the basis of this booklet, was provided by Tiana Woods. Initial editing and proofreading were provided by Valerie Fullilove. The print ready cover graphics and interior formatting were provided by Word & Spirit Publishing. The cover design, concept, and art direction were provided by Julio Vitolo.

Scripture quotations marked (KJV) are taken from the King James Version Bible. Public Domain.

Scripture quotations marked (NKJV) are taken from the New King James Version®. Copyright © 1982 by Thomas Nelson. Used by permission. All rights reserved.

Scripture quotations marked (ESV) are taken from The Holy Bible, English Standard Version® (ESV®), Copyright © 2001 by Crossway, a publishing ministry of Good News Publishers. Used by permission. All rights reserved.

Scripture quotations marked (NIV) are taken from The Holy Bible, New International Version®, NIV®. Copyright © 1973, 1978, 1984, 2011 by Biblica, Inc.® Used by permission of Zondervan. All rights reserved worldwide. www.zondervan.com. The NIV and New International Version are trademarks registered in the United States Patent and Trademark Office by Biblica, Inc. TM

Scripture quotations marked (NASB) are taken from the New American Standard Bible®, Copyright © 1960, 1962, 1963, 1968, 1971, 1972, 1973, 1975, 1977, 1995 by The Lockman Foundation. Used by permission. (www.Lockman.org)

Scripture quotations marked (NLT) are taken from the Holy Bible, New Living Translation, Copyright © 1996, 2004, 2015 by Tyndale House Foundation. Used by permission of Tyndale House Publishers, Inc., Carol Stream, Illinois 60188. All rights reserved.

Scripture quotations marked (AMP) are taken from the Amplified® Bible, Copyright © 2015 by The Lockman Foundation. Used by permission. (www.Lockman.org.). All rights reserved.

Scripture quotations marked (BSB) are taken from the Berean Study Bible. The Holy Bible, Berean Study Bible, BSB. Copyright ©2016, 2020 by Bible Hub. Used by permission. All rights reserved worldwide.

Cover images are used by permission of Shutterstock: acqua_colore & Astro Ann, Shutterstock.com

ISBN: 978-1-7357880-3-6

Published by Word and Spirit Publishing
P.O Box 701403, Tulsa Oklahoma 74170
wordandspiritpublishing.com

in connection with Gale Alvarez, Love of Jesus Ministries, Inc,
448 Highland Avenue, Orange, NJ 07050

GALEALVAREZ.COM

CONTENTS

FOREWORD

During the early days of the pandemic, Pastor Gale Alvarez was inspired to deliver a fresh word of encouragement to her church family and to her Facebook Live viewers. As the days progressed, Gale began to name the days of the week to focus on the special thoughts God graciously gave to her. One Tuesday, Gale named her day, "Thrive Tuesday" and henceforth, the title "Thrive with God."

Gale is passionate about bringing all people, believers and non-believers, to a place of purpose, fullness, and abundance through the goodness and grace of God. Through a lens of piercing disappointments and personal losses, Gale has realized that through our own efforts little can be accomplished, but with the help of God, we can go from a surviving state of mind to a thriving lifestyle filled with God's glory and with God's unfailing, empowering, and merciful love.

In order to thrive, Gale tells us that we need to, *"connect in the disconnect"* regardless of the season we find ourselves in. Through her own quest to thrive, Gale emphasizes that we absolutely cannot do it alone, but with God, we can experience a supernatural power to live a life of hope, victory, and fulfillment. In the pages of this book, Gale will bring to life some practical yet profound ways to connect to the all-powerful, eternal life source of a loving, caring God.

I say to the Lord, "You are my Lord;
apart from you I have no good thing."

(Psalm 16:2 NIV)

INTRODUCTION

THRIVE—it's not a word used often, and I wonder if we even fully know what it means. Life is quite an adventure with many challenges along the way, and many times our focus is on surviving the journey rather than thriving in each of our destinations within life's journey. I believe we need to come to a place in life where we seek to thrive daily. The definition of thrive is: to prosper, to flourish, to grow, to level up, to bloom, to be fruitful, and to increase. I like that! In the beginning, didn't God give us a directive and His blessing when He said, "Be fruitful and multiply"? (see Genesis 1:28) The secret to our thriving is realizing that with God's help we can thrive in this world.

I also like that the word thrive is a state of mind and an action word; meaning we need to take action and be aware that there's more to life than just surviving. We need to level up, accept the help of God, and start thriving.

There are lots of conflicts in life that try to defeat us; yet, we can flourish and thrive in each one of them if we stay connected to the vine— to God's unfailing love and unlimited power.

It is my prayer that as you read the pages and God's promises in this book, you will take heart, receive hope, be encouraged, and change your thinking from Survive to Thrive. I LOVE YOU, Gale.

Beloved, I wish above all things that thou mayest prosper and be in health, even as thy soul prospereth.

(3 John 1:2 KJV)

Thrive Tuesday

SURVIVE OR THRIVE

**Then God blessed them, and God said
to them, "Be fruitful and multiply;
fill the earth and subdue it;"
(Genesis 1:28 NKJV)**

Hello, happy Tuesday. Wow, I'm surprised I even remembered it was Tuesday. It's been a little bit rough remembering what day it is lately, but today is Tuesday, so happy Tuesday.

Last night I went shopping to get a few things I needed from the grocery store. Thank God they had most of what I needed. I needed fresh vegetables and some healthy food choices.

I'm trying to fill up on good survival food these days for better health and well-being. So, as I was shopping, I began to think about survival skills. Earlier I was talking to one of the youth leaders, and I remembered he is an Eagle Scout. To me, that's impressive. I thought about this for a while; it takes a lot of skill to become eligible for the rank of Eagle Scout, and climbing those hills isn't easy, but it is possible with the right attitude and discipline. When I came home, I took out my journal like I normally do, and I wrote the words, "Survival Skills." When I woke up this morning, survival was still heavy on my heart, and then the thought came, "Survival Skills for the Christian Life." But, after thinking about this for a while, I decided to change the title "Survival Skills" to "Thriving Skills" because I believe God doesn't want us to just survive: He wants us to thrive. He wants us to blossom and bloom abundantly. He wants us to continue to grow, grow, and grow some more.

Do you realize a seed in the ground has to push through a lot of dirt to grow up to become a flower that gives fragrance to the people or things that come around it? I know many of us are feeling life's pressures right now. It feels like there's dirt on top of the seed inside of us. But just like the flower, by the grace of God we've got to push through. We must realize that the Spirit of God is helping us right now to push through, and therefore, it's best for us to believe we will continue growing even in this season. With God's help we will surely thrive. Say it, believe it, and then act on it. ***"With God's help we will surely thrive."*** You will be amazed how that seed of greatness will thrive in you because it's what God promises to His children.

*Bless the Lord, O my soul, and all that is within me, bless his holy name!
Bless the Lord, O my soul, and forget not all his benefits, who forgives all your iniquity, who heals all your diseases, who redeems your life from the pit, who crowns you with steadfast love and mercy, who satisfies you with good so that your youth is renewed like the eagle's.*

(Psalm 103:1–5 ESV)

So, on this morning, I just want to drop some thoughts on you about thriving skills in every season. These are not just for the Christian life, but for any life. First, we need to ask ourselves, what skills are we nurturing right now in order to thrive in this season? It's important to have a vision, a plan, and to know God's heart for you. Let's think about the sun. We all know that in the natural world we need the sunshine and all of its many benefits. When the sun doesn't shine, we miss the sunshine and all the goodness it has to offer.

But for those of us who know the Lord, we have the goodness of the S-O-N, Jesus; the Son of God lives on the inside of us. With the S-O-N, we have His Word, His promises, and His love. We also have Him, we have His Holy Spirit, we have hope, and we have Christ in us, the hope of Glory. *(see Colossians 1:27 KJV).*

I can do all things through Christ who strengthens me.

(Philippians 4:13 NKJV)

I pray that out of his glorious riches he may strengthen you with power through his Spirit in your inner being, so that Christ may dwell in your hearts through faith.

(Ephesians 3:16–17 NIV)

Knowing that Christ lives in us, we can always have God's care and loving sunshine through His S-O-N and through His Word. Scripture teaches us that the entrance of His Word brings light, and we know that Jesus is the "Word of God" (see John 1:1–5, 14) and the "Light of the world" (see John 8:12).

*The entrance of Your words gives light;
It gives understanding to the simple.*

(Psalm 119:130 NKJV)

*In the beginning was the Word,
and the Word was with God,
and the Word was God. . . .
In him was life, and that life
was the light of all mankind.
The light shines in the darkness,
and the darkness has not overcome it.*

(John 1:1,4–5 NIV)

What a wonderful gift. We can walk in the light; we can walk in God's sunshine today. We can gain supernatural wisdom to gain victory in all of life's affairs. There is no darkness that we will not be able to overcome as we fellowship with God's S-O-N light. The light of God's Word will show us things to come and open up avenues of spiritual and natural opportunities we have not yet known. We will experience the warmth of God's love and know the assurance of His hope even on the darkest day.

Call to Me, and I will answer you, and show you great and mighty things, which you do not know.

(Jeremiah 33:3 NKJV)

For some of us, it's become a little dark in this season. It's become difficult to get through, difficult to see the light. But I can tell you today that if you will just open your hearts to the Word of God, the entrance of His Word will bring you light. It will bring you a new awareness that God is with you, fighting your battles and guiding you into fields of abundance. God's light refreshes; it lifts, encourages, and brings us new hope. God's light will open your eyes to His unfailing love in every situation and in every season. You will feel a new confidence, a new power, a renewed love in His light because you will know you are not alone.

For the fountain of life is with You;
In Your light we see light.

(Psalm 36:9 NASB)

Open your heart wide. Open God's Word today. Allow the Son, the S-O-N, to shine into those places where you've been struggling. I know you're struggling, I understand. God Himself understands the struggle. He wants you to know that He is your ever-present help in your time of need. Regardless of the need, God's grace and unfailing love will reach you where no one else has ever been able to reach you. The entrance of God's Word is like medicine, it will heal; it will penetrate your innermost being and make old things new. It will bring you joy where there once was sadness, hope where there once was no hope. It will bring His forgiving love that never fails.

He reveals the deep things of darkness
and brings deep shadows into light.

(Job 12:22 BSB)

And when you receive God's merciful, healing love, you will be blessed with an overflowing joy, and it can take you to places where you can be sunshine in the life of another. He'll lead you to where you can be a love light in someone else's life. Just talking to our youth leader today was a light for me, a moment of love, a moment of refreshing. Let's always share with great compassion the love and light we receive.

The LORD has appeared of old to me, saying: "Yes, I have loved you with an everlasting love; Therefore with lovingkindness I have drawn you."

(Jeremiah 31:3 NKJV)

How precious is your unfailing love, O God! All humanity finds shelter in the shadow of your wings.

(Psalm 36:7 NLT)

I often speak to friends who have children. We text each other, and I see the passion and purpose continuing to press and push forth in these parents, even in this difficult season. They are strengthened by their purpose to be good, providing parents, just like Jesus was strengthened by His purpose to give us life. As I have been given an opportunity to help them, the beauty of God's love pours forth into my life. I get lifted, I get refreshed, and I feel connected to eternity in the process. In this sharing, I see God's light and I feel His love. Don't lose your purpose. Don't lose your passion. Be sunshine today in the life of another. This will bring you life, and it will bring them life. Speak a word of love and light to someone today. Let the comfort you have received be poured out as comfort into the life of someone else today.

Praise be to the God and Father
of our Lord Jesus Christ,
the Father of compassion
and the God of all comfort,
who comforts us in all our troubles,
so that we can comfort those
in any trouble with the comfort
we ourselves receive from God.

(2 Corinthians 1:3–4, NIV)

He Satisfies Our Needs

But my God shall supply all your need according to his riches in glory by Christ Jesus.

(Philippians 4:19 KJV)

What else do we need to do to thrive today, to thrive in this season, to thrive in any and every season?

We need the Bread of Life. Jesus said if we eat of His bread, it will satisfy our hunger. We have empty places that can only be satisfied by Jesus, by our fellowship with Him. Yes, I know we need food. Can I tell you I'm a little bit tired of eating plain peanut butter and jelly sandwiches? So last night, I got some celery, and I decided to put my peanut butter in the celery. Then I remembered that back in the day I used to create what looked like ants on a log, where I would put peanut butter on my celery and top it with raisins. It really looked like ants on a log. I used to do that for the kids, but today, I did it for me because I needed something good that would brighten my day.

For He satisfies the longing soul,
And fills the hungry soul with goodness.

(Psalm 107:9 NKJV)

Jesus said to them, "Very truly I tell you, it is not Moses who has given you the bread from heaven, but it is my Father who gives you the true bread from heaven. For the bread of God is the bread that comes down from heaven and gives life to the world."

(John 6:32–33 NIV)

Now that we have Jesus, the Bread of Life, what else do we need to thrive? We need water. Every day I drink so much water. I always have water with me. But as much as water quenches my thirst in the natural, it can never quench the dryness that tries to come inside of us when we're in dry seasons. The good news is that we can stay wet and quenched even in the dry seasons. We stay wet by the washing of God's Word—the living water that lasts forever. His eternal water brings life, it cleanses, and it refreshes. It causes us not to be thirsty again. But, if you stay out of the water, away from His Word, you're going to get thirsty. If you don't drink the water of His Word, if you don't begin to say and remind yourselves of God's promises like in Psalm 1:3, you will become dry. Psalm 1:3 says, *"That person is like a tree planted by streams of water, which yields its fruit in season and whose leaf does not wither—whatever they do prospers"* (NIV). When you believe, speak, and act on God's promises, you will thrive with God's grace in any dry season. God bless you!

As the deer pants for streams of water, so my soul longs after You, O God.

(Psalm 42:1 BSB)

Jesus replied, "I am the bread of life. Whoever comes to me will never be hungry again. Whoever believes in me will never be thirsty."

(John 6:35 NLT)

Only the living water of His Word can make you thrive and flourish, so you never thirst again. It's not possible to just drink water now and then and expect to blossom. No, let's drink living water all the time. When we drench ourselves in God's Word, we become replenished, we flourish, and we thrive. Being soaked in God's water is vital for me. When I don't have it, I feel it. It's time for us to understand that if we're not hungering and thirsting after His righteousness, we are not going to be filled. We need to go to the well, the well that provides all grace, all hope, and everything we need to thrive.

"Blessed are they which do hunger and thirst after righteousness: for they shall be filled."

(Matthew 5:6 KJV)

The eyes of all look expectantly to You, And You give them their food in due season. You open Your hand And satisfy the desire of every living thing.

(Psalm 145:15–16 NKJV)

I pray that you are inspired today to go to the well and drink of God's living water. For us to experience the amazing benefits God has for us, in the here and now and for eternity, we need to drink of His living waters and of His unfailing love found only in His Holy Word.

Jesus answered, "Everyone who drinks this water will be thirsty again, but whoever drinks the water I give them will never thirst. Indeed, the water I give them will become in them a spring of water welling up to eternal life."

(John 4:13–14 NIV)

When we receive God's Word into our lives, as promised, we will also be filled with the Spirit and life of Christ to live abundantly—to not just survive but to thrive in all seasons. Our hearts will overflow with God's pure love, and we will become a fountain of love pouring into others who need a touch from a loving God.

Praise, Worship, and Thrive

You make known to me the path of life;
in your presence there is fullness of joy;
at your right hand are
pleasures forevermore.

(Psalm 16:11 ESV)

Another way we thrive and flourish is through our praise and worship. There's not a moment in these times when I don't have music playing. It's either playing on my phone in my pocket as I do work around my house, or it's playing somewhere on a speaker. Last night, around eight o'clock, I knew there was a curfew where I couldn't go riding around. So, you know what I did? I got into my car, I turned on the ignition, and I blasted my music till it launched me into a glorious place of worship and praise.

I began to sing spontaneous, blessed, holy words from Psalm 119: "Forever, Forever Lord, Your Word is settled. Forever, Forever Lord, Your Word is settled in heaven. Forever Lord, Forever Lord." And I just kept singing and finding myself in the midst of God's penetrating presence. I was filled, I was there with the Lord, and I was thriving. It seems when you find that secret place with God, whatever seemed so overwhelming is now something you can give to God and have the confidence that all will be well. SO BE IT, SO BE IT, ALL WILL BE WELL. The Lord's Word is settled, and He is faithful to me, faithful to you, and faithful to those who trust and believe in Him and in the abundant life He promises in HIS WORD. That's my "SO BE IT." I ask you this day: What are the "SO BE ITS" in your life? Don't let go of them now; God is forever faithful. Thrive, thrive, thrive. Thrive with God. Believe God, and believe in God's Word. Find His presence, and let His Word be your "SO BE IT."

Forever, O Lord,
your word is settled in heaven.
Your faithfulness endures
to all generations;
you established the earth,
and it abides.

(Psalm 119:89–90 NKJV)

Connect in the Disconnect

"Again I say to you, if two of you agree on earth about anything they ask, it will be done for them by my Father in heaven. For where two or three are gathered in my name, there am I among them."

(Matthew 18:19–20 ESV)

We also need each other to thrive. Thankfully, we're living in an age of technology where we can stay connected in the disconnect. Right now, we've experienced some disconnection because things are not the way they used to be. Not being able to go out to do the things we normally do is not normal; it causes a disconnect, but there doesn't have to be a disconnect in community. We are connected through cell phones, through FaceTime, through live personal broadcasts, through greeting cards, and through Zoom meetings; we are connected through so many things. Don't allow yourself to feel disconnected in the disconnect, instead— plug in.

The human body has many parts, but the many parts make up one whole body. So it is with the body of Christ. But our bodies have many parts, and God has put each part just where he wants it. How strange a body would be if it had only one part! Yes, there are many parts, but only one body. The eye can never say to the hand, "I don't need you." The head can't say to the feet, "I don't need you." In fact, some parts of the body that seem weakest and least important are actually the most necessary.

(1 Corinthians 12:12, 18–22 NLT)

First and foremost, plug into God. Plug Him into the areas in your life where the enemy is coming against you to make you feel alone and isolated. You are never alone. The Lord says in His Word, *"I am with you always, even unto the end of the world." (Matthew 28:20 KJV)*. His Word also tells us that He will be our portion forever (see Psalm 73:26). He will! What is the portion that you need from Him today? *"Ask, and it will be given to you; seek, and you will find; knock, and it will be opened to you." (Matthew 7:7 NKJV)*. So many of us have not because we ask not. Ask Him. Ask others. Let what you need be known unto God. Let it be known unto the community of faith so that we can help you.

> *"...you must help the weak and remember the words of the Lord Jesus, that He Himself said, 'It is more blessed to give than to receive.'"*
>
> **(Acts 20:35 NASB)**

Let us then approach the throne of grace with confidence, so that we may receive mercy and find grace to help us in our time of need.

(Hebrews 4:16 BSB)

We are here to help; we are here to serve. The Bible tells us that Jesus *"did not come to be served, but to serve" (Matthew 20:28 NIV)*. Too many of us are waiting around for someone to serve us when God has called us to be servants to others. Serve in any capacity you can right now. Shine in the capacity that you are gifted to shine in. It can be anything that helps someone in need. Your capacity is greater than you know. You have greatness in you. You are stronger than you know. It's just like a car; you have to turn it on to get the power. Last night, I had to turn on my car and then my audio system to fill my car and fill myself with songs of deliverance and songs of hope. I had to do something, and when I did, God was with me in my action, and my action lifted me because God was in it. God is forever with you. That action of turning on the radio blessed me; those songs encouraged me, challenged me, and changed me. When I came back into my house, my husband said, *"Where were you? You have a skip in your step tonight."* Yes, I did have a skip. I was skipping on the inside just because I got away. I sat in my car, in my driveway, I turned the power on, and just got lost in God's worship and praise. I became lost in God's presence. What are you doing to thrive in this time—in this season? What are you turning on? How are you thriving? Thrive in the name of Jesus.

Another area where I believe we can thrive is by taking communion every day. The Bible tells us to take communion in remembrance of Him. When we take of the bread and drink of the wine, we are remembering Jesus: His body that was broken and His blood that was shed to set us free. We also remember that He was raised from the dead to give us a New Life. Yes, we need to remember these elements now more than ever. When you take communion with your friends, you will enjoy the fellowship and the unique connection you share with each other and with Jesus, the Son of God. There is something supernatural that happens when we take communion. A special, sweet, and holy presence of God is released into our lives that also reminds us of our freedom and newness in Christ. We are reminded that we are forgiven, set free from guilt, set free from addictions, set free from sin, set free from condemnation, and set free from old patterns that hold us back in life. An amazing grace comes to us when we engage in communion. We are reminded of our new life in Christ. The apostle Paul tells us about this new life:

*This means that anyone who belongs
to Christ has become a new person.
The old life is gone; a new life has begun!*

(2 Corinthians 5:17 NLT)

Connect in the Disconnect

I have been crucified with Christ and I no longer live, but Christ lives in me. The life I now live in the body, I live by faith in the Son of God, who loved me and gave himself for me.

(Galatians 2:20 NIV)

I talked to a friend this week, and we set up a Zoom meeting to do communion with our children's church teachers and our helpers who are trying so hard to continue to be a presence in the lives of our kids. Taking communion encouraged us, brought us together, and connected us to thrive in the disconnect.

There's a community for you to connect with—to help today. Will you be the sunshine to your community? Will you be a light? Will you be bread to them? Will you bring living water to them with words that speak life and light to them? Maybe you are the one who's lacking today, and maybe you are the one who needs to be lifted more than anyone else. You might be surprised that the phone call you make today, rather than sitting around waiting for someone else to call you, might be exactly what you need to start your engine—to turn on your faucet of life.

"Give, and it will be given to you.
A good measure, pressed down,
shaken together, and running over
will be poured into your lap.
For with the measure you use,
it will be measured back to you."

(Luke 6:38 BSB)

Today Is the Day

This is the day the Lord has made;
We will rejoice and be glad in it.

(Psalm 118:24 NKJV)

Start your engine today. Thrive in this season. Today I remind you of the power and possibilities you have with Jesus, and I say: *"Let God arise, let his enemies be scattered" (Psalm 68:1 KJV).*

"Don't be dejected and sad,
for the joy of the LORD
is your strength!"

(Nehemiah 8:10 NLT)

*In conclusion, be strong in the Lord
[draw your strength from Him
and be empowered through
your union with Him] and in the
power of His [boundless] might.*

(Ephesians 6:10 AMP)

*"So do not worry about tomorrow;
for tomorrow will worry about itself."*

(Matthew 6:34 NASB)

Thrive Today In This Season. Thrive Today. Just Focus On Today and Thrive Today. Do What You Can Do Today.

His grace is sufficient for you today. In every single day there is renewed grace and mercy that's sufficient for us for the day. Yes, there are days when I want to say, "You know what God, can I just have a scoop of tomorrow's grace today?" No, it doesn't work that way. His grace is sufficient for today. So, I pray today that you would allow His grace to be sufficient for you. I pray that His Word would be a light for you, and I pray that you would reach out and be a light to someone else. I pray you would let the sunshine in, and then go out and shine on others. You can shine in so many ways. You can shine through your phone, shine at your desk, or shine through a greeting card. Shine and be sunshine to someone's life today. It will bless you, and it will bless them.

Stay connected with God, connect with friends, and don't get lost in the shuffle. Stay in the community of faith. We are here for you. We love you. We're praying for you, and we are here to serve you even now. So, if there's something we can do for you or if you have a prayer request, let us know. Remember to take communion and no excuses. You don't have juice? Okay, use water. You don't even have to use bread and water. I had grapes delivered to me today from a very efficient company. So today, I'm going to get to do communion with bread and grapes. This will represent the blood and the body of Jesus that was broken and shed for me. I encourage you to remember the Lord today. Remember all of what He did for you and all of who He was and is. Remember what you've been taught. Remember what you know. Continue to walk in the light you have received and allow your light to be increased. Become sunshine; be sunshine.

"Soon the world will no longer see me,
but you will see me.
Since I live, you also will live.
When I am raised to life again,
you will know that I am in my Father,
and you are in me, and I am in you."

(John 14:19–20 NLT)

Again Jesus spoke to them, saying,
"I am the light of the world.
Whoever follows me will not walk in
darkness, but will have the light of life."

(John 8:12 ESV)

I love you. I'm praying for you. I pray that you would stay encouraged; I pray that you would stay faith filled with the power of God's love and with the assurance of God's infinite ability. Let go of your limited ability and accept His New Life—accept the God of no limits. Remember the words of Jesus:

And looking at them, Jesus said to them, "With people this is impossible, but with God all things are possible."

(Matthew 19:26 NASB)

The only way you can stay faithful and apprehend the love and ability of God is to stay faith filled. God is pleased by your faith, pleased that you believe in Him, and pleased with your faithfulness. So, drink the water of God's Word—of His promises today. Become refreshed; allow Him to be your portion. His grace is sufficient for you today. He offers His free gift to you. He has you covered. I love you. Have a beautiful day. God bless you.

*If God is for us,
who can be against us?*

(Romans 8:31 NKJV)

Eight "So Be It" Promises to Help You Thrive

Very simply, the number 8 in Scripture represents a new beginning. The number 8 can represent a new way of thinking, a new way of living, a new way of loving, and a new way of experiencing the love and power of God in your life to **thrive and to fulfill your God-given destiny.**

Connect with God today and go from Survive to Thrive.

I pray that you will find a new intimacy with God and receive His Word like a love letter guiding you and giving you inspiration and hope to go the next mile—to the next level of awareness in your journey. May the Lord's hope, guidance, ability, grace, and love always be with you. And remember the ever-present words of Jesus:

Jesus answered, "It is written: 'Man shall not live on bread alone, but on every word that comes from the mouth of God.'"

(Matthew 4:4 NIV)

"As the Father hath loved me, so have I loved you: continue ye in my love."

(John 15:9 KJV)

"Peace I leave with you, My peace I give to you; not as the world gives do I give to you. Let not your heart be troubled, neither let it be afraid."

(John 14:27 NKJV)

I pray you find comfort and strength in God's powerful Words of promise. Allow God's Words to become part of your every step, your every thought, and your every breath. God created us and knows what's most fruitful in every situation of our lives. His desire is for you to prosper. Jesus reminds us that if we believe in His ability and not our own, we can speak to circumstances and see supernatural change that otherwise would not be possible. **The emphasis is believing and connecting with God's ability and not our own. Jesus said this to His disciples:**

"Have faith in God." . . .
"Truly I tell you, if anyone says to this mountain, 'Go, throw yourself into the sea,' and does not doubt in their heart but believes that what they say will happen, it will be done for them."

(Mark 11:22–23 NIV)

So today, I leave you with the symbolic number of 8 promises from the thousands of precious promises in God's Word as you venture in your new beginning from glory to glory—from Survive to Thrive.

Connect with God. Believe God's Word. Speak God's Word.

I love you, Gale Alvarez.

Eight Promises
for You

*And God is able to make
all grace abound to you,
so that in all things, at all times,
having all that you need,
you will abound in
every good work.*

(2 Corinthians 9:8 BSB)

Do not be anxious about anything,
but in everything by prayer and
supplication with thanksgiving let
your requests be made known to God.
And the peace of God, which surpasses
all understanding, will guard your
hearts and your minds in Christ Jesus.

(Philippians 4:6–7 ESV)

Delight yourself also in the Lord,
And He shall give you
the desires of your heart.

(Psalm 37:4 NKJV)

The LORD will always guide you;
He will satisfy you in a sun-scorched land
and strengthen your frame.
You will be like a well-watered garden,
like a spring whose waters never fail.

(Isaiah 58:11 BSB)

*The steadfast love of the Lord
never ceases; his mercies never come
to an end; they are new every morning;
great is your faithfulness.
"The Lord is my portion," says my soul,
"therefore I will hope in him."*

(Lamentations 3:22–24 ESV)

*His divine power has given us everything
we need for life and godliness through
the knowledge of Him who called us
by His own glory and excellence.*

(2 Peter 1:3 BSB)

*"For I know the plans I have for you,"
declares the LORD, "plans to prosper
you and not to harm you, plans to
give you hope and a future."*

(Jeremiah 29:11 NIV)

Thus says the LORD, your Redeemer, The Holy One of Israel: "I am the LORD your God, Who teaches you to profit, Who leads you by the way you should go."

(Isaiah 48:17 NKJV)

About the Author

GALE ALVAREZ

"Thirty years of dedicated, hands-to-the-plow ministry as co-founder and co-pastor of the Love of Jesus Family Church, combined with ten thousand hidden acts of kindness that multitudes and heaven know of, are the treasures that make up the precious woman of God, Gale Alvarez.

Inside and outside of her church, Gale delivers the Word of God with compassion, prophetic precision, and timely accuracy. Outside of the sanctuary walls, she lives her life in selfless abandonment, giving her time and sharing her resources, her pure faith, and her love to the masses of humanity with whom she comes into contact. Her devotion is endless, and her heart is wide open to receive from God as she gives back to others.

Thank you, Gale, for displaying the beauty that only He can make from the ashes of our lives. Thank you for being an example of a living sacrifice. I am honored to know her and to be loved by her and to share in life's journey together.

~ **Dr. Dawn Chillon, PhD, LPC, Founder - The Foundation for Family Healing**

"Gale Alvarez pours out of her very being and her life experience to engage people where they live."

~ **Valerie J. Fullilove, Writer/ Producer - Trinity Park Productions**

"Pastor Gale is a visionary with integrity and sterling character. From her gentle elegance, but firm, confident voice, flow volumes of wisdom."

~ Bettye Blackston -
The Women of Purpose Ministry

"The healing ointment that comes from Gale's special journey is a sweet savor to God."

~ Dr. Gerald G. Lloyd -
Fountain of Life
International Fellowship

"If you sit more than two minutes with Gale, you will hear the heartbeat of God."

~ Reverend Pat Higgins -
Restoration Family Church,
Hillside, New Jersey

"Gale Alvarez is a woman who puts her actions where her intentions are—just amazing."

> ~ **Pastor Cassiaus Farrell,**
> **Founder - The Love of Jesus**
> **Family Church,**
> **Patterson, New Jersey**

"There has never been a time when Pastor Gale hasn't spoken directly to my heart. We are thankful for her compassion, commitment, and dedication to the people of God."

> ~ **Bishop Barbara Glanton,**
> **Pastor - The Love of Jesus**
> **Family Church,**
> **Newark, New Jersey**

"It is evident that Gale has taken the circumstances that life has served her as opportunities to find God and ever press into a greater love and knowledge of the Most High!"

> ~ **Barry E. Taylor, Founder -**
> **Liberty Ministries Inc.**

Pastor Gale's Website:

www.GaleAlvarez.com

Pastor Gale's Facebook Pages:

Gale Alvarez HeartBeats & Gale Alvarez

YouTube: Gale Alvarez

Gale is available for speaking engagements and can be contacted at: 973-676-4200

An overwhelming, special thanks to all the precious "sounding boards" for the countless hours they spent on this project. May the Lord richly bless them and return to them the favor, time, grace, commitment, and effort they have freely given to make "Thrive with God" a special reality in the lives of the readers.

GALE'S ENERGIZING AND THOUGHTFUL DEVOTIONALS

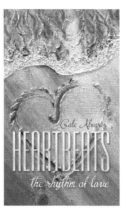

"I am forever changed by His love."
—Gale Alvarez

*So shall My word be that
goes forth from My mouth;
It shall not return to Me void,
But it shall accomplish
what I please, And it shall
prosper in the thing
for which I sent it.*

(Isaiah 55:11 NKJV)